Just

: A Story of Justice and Redemption

by Bryan Stevenson

: This is a quick read summary based on the book

"Just Mercy"

by Bryan Stevenson

TABLE OF CONTENTS

Overview

SUMMARY

Epilogue

ANALYSIS

OVERVIEW

This review of Just Mercy: A Story of Justice and Redemption, by Bryan Stevenson, provides a chapter by chapter detailed summary followed by an analysis and critique of the strengths and weaknesses of the book.

The main theme explored in the book is the injustice of our criminal justice system. The author uses the case of Walter McMillian's wrongful conviction of murder and imprisonment as an overarching example of how the U.S. justice system does not prosecute fairly. The author focuses on how race, socioeconomic status, and even age have an effect on how certain criminals are convicted.

Stevenson uses his personal experience as a lawyer for the Equal Justice Initiative and more than 25 years fighting for the rights of people who could not afford legal counsel as a basis for this novel. Through his own experiences, the author makes the case that it is often the people on the fringe of society who need proper justice and mercy, and yet, they are the ones who are least likely to receive it. By sharing his own case work, the author demonstrates how unjust death penalty convictions have been over the past fifty years and how hard it is to truly make change in the system.

The central thesis of the work is that we are more than the worst things we have done. Yet, we live in a country that will, on the basis of one poor choice or decision, condemn a person to life in prison, or worse, death. Even further, law enforcement often targets those who have neither the money nor education to fight back, and this has had a direct correlation to the rise in mass incarceration over the past century. The author's purpose is to shine a light on this and bring about the kind of change that uses mercy as its own form of justice.

Bryan Stevenson is a lawyer, social justice activist, and the founder of the Equal Justice Initiative. He attended Eastern University and graduated in 1981. After that he attended

Harvard Law School where he found his career calling by working for the Southern Center for Human Rights. He has since traveled the country, working for EJI, and speaking about the politics and social injustice of the prison system and death penalty. 2/23/19

SUMMARY

INTRODUCTION: HIGHER GROUND

Stevenson begins his novel in 1983, when he was a twenty-three year old law student at Harvard and had just taken an internship in Georgia at a maximum security prison. He goes back in his own life, explaining how he came to that moment. When he graduated from college with a degree in philosophy, he quickly realized that there was nothing he could do in his field of study and chose law school as the most reasonable choice post-graduation. At the time he had absolutely no interest in law, but he knew that he wanted to help people, specifically poor people and those who faced racial inequality in America.

The summer after his first year of law school brought him to a juvenile justice program in Philadelphia and this encouraged him to enroll in a one month intensive course on race and poverty litigation during his second year at Harvard. One of the requirements of this class was to spend the month with an organization doing social justice work and that is how he found himself working with the Southern Prisoners Defense Committee in 1983.

Stevenson describes the social climate of prisons at the time, particularly how executions were becoming more prevalent in the Deep South. The program he was working with, the SPDC, was receiving frantic calls daily from prisoners who had no legal assistance and were facing rapidly approaching dates of execution. This was how he found himself, one day, heading to one of the more notorious prisons in Georgia to visit a man that no other lawyer had time to visit. This man, named Henry, had been on death row for two years and still had not been provided legal assistance. Upon meeting Henry, the author is struck by the man's compassion, generosity, and pure graciousness. This altered the way the author viewed humanity's potential and he returned to Harvard with a newfound desire to understand the laws that allow the death penalty and extreme punishments of prisoners in our country.

Stevenson explains that during his time working on death row, he began to understand that there was something missing in our judicial system that allowed us to treat certain prisoners unfairly. This, he explains, was something he had struggled to understand his whole life: why are certain people treated unfairly? The author's intentions in writing this book are to take a close look at mass incarceration and extreme forms of punishment in America. He previews how he will look at how easily we condemn people in America and how the makeup of death row prisoners is reflective of America's own racial and social fears and prejudices.

Returning to his own narrative, he explains that after law school he returned to the Deep South to begin a program to help represent the poor, incarcerated, and unjustly condemned. He previews one particular man, Walter McMillian, whom he will follow over the course of the book as a means to describe what he has learned about our system's indifference to inaccurate and unfair prosecutions. Despite the darkness in the pages to come, the author hints that McMillian's case, as well as several others that he will also document, will also show that there is a light. These stories demonstrate that we are more than the worst things we have done and the true measure of our country's commitment to justice is how we treat the poor, accused, incarcerated, and condemned. 2/23/19

CHAPTER ONE: MOCKINGBIRD PLAYERS

Stevenson begins the narrative shortly after he was assigned Walter McMillian's case and received a phone call from Judge Robert E. Lee Key. During the call, Judge Key cautioned Stevenson not to take the case, warning him about the depravity of the man he was about to defend, even suggesting that he might be a part of the "Dixie Mafia." At this point, the author was in his late twenties and had been working with the SPDC for four years. He and his friend Eva Ansley had recently decided to create a new nonprofit organization that would represent people on death row. In preparation for opening this new organization, Stevenson met with five condemned men in Alabama: Willie Tabb, Vernon Madison, Jesse Morrison, Harry Nicks, and Walter McMillian. Despite his own overwhelming sense of exhaustion, the author distinctly remembers how insistent McMillian was during their initial meeting that he was wrongfully convicted and admits that he was inclined to believe his client until proven otherwise.

Stevenson delves into the historical background of Alabama in the 1960's through the 1980's and parallels it with the region's most famous novel: Harper Lee's *To Kill a Mockingbird*. This sets the stage for the injustices he is about to share for the reader as he carefully points out that many people forget that the poor, condemned black prisoner of the novel does not reach a happy end.

The author next examines Walter McMillian's personal history, and how he found himself on Alabama's death row. Tracing his success through the 1970's and 80's in creating his own pulpwood business, Stevenson underlines a thread of racism in his hometown of Monroeville and how they treated McMillian's independence with suspicion and contempt. For the white people in that town, McMillian was achieving beyond what he should have and, despite being pleasant and professional, many in the community would have liked to have seen him fail.

What ultimately brought McMillian to his incarceration, the author explains, was his reputation as a ladies' man. Despite being married with three children, he had engaged in several extramarital affairs and it was one of these affairs—with a white woman named Karen Kelly—that proved to be his undoing. The scandal surrounding their relationship—even during the time period of the 1980's, where interracial relationships should not have been such a big deal—led to the community's public disgrace of Kelly, her husband, and McMillian.

McMillian was subpoenaed to speak during the custody hearings of the Kellys' children and this brought up old fears of interracial relationships in this Deep Southern community. Stevenson explains that it was not until 1967 that the U.S. Supreme Court struck down anti-miscegenation laws and by 1986—when Kelly and McMillian had been involved—there were still many restrictions on interracial relationships. Many black men had been lynched in Alabama, particularly in their own Monroe County, for engaging with white women, and this obviously had bearing on how the community viewed McMillian.

In November of 1986, the eighteen year old daughter of one of Monroeville's most prominent families was found murdered. Due to the scarcity of murders in their town, and the sheer horror of what was done to the young woman, the community was up in arms to find her killer. The police attempted to track down all possible leads, taking them both in and out of the community, but to no avail. After several months without a suspect, the public began to criticize the police.

While this was occurring, McMillian was preoccupied with trying to end his relationship with Kelly. Kelly had begun using drugs heavily and started to associate with a man named Ralph Myers. Together, they became involved in drug dealing and became suspects in the murder of a young woman from a neighboring county, Vickie Lynn Pittman. Under questioning by the police, Ralph Myers denied his own involvements and attempted to pin the murder on other members of the community, eventually leading him to finger Kelly and her boyfriend McMillian as the murderers of Pittman. Even further, Myers claimed that McMillian was also responsible for the murder of Ronda Morrison, the eighteen year old from Monroeville. Seven months had passed since her murder and the police were desperate to provide the ever-angering public with a suspect. So, despite being unable to prove that Myers knew McMillian, let alone that they had ever met or that Myer's testimony was true, the Monroe County Sheriff Tom Tate used his witness's statements, as well as the history of McMillian's infamous interracial affair, as grounds to arrest McMillian for Morrison's murder.   2/24/19

CHAPTER TWO: STAND

By the time Stevenson had taken on McMillian's case he had been working admittedly insane hours driving back and forth from Atlanta to Alabama in attempting to get his new non-profit up and running. He explains that the intensity of his work paralleled the worsening conditions for prisoners across the country. In the aftermath of Attica Prison riots in the 1970s, America had been exposed to the dangers of prison abuse and the inhuman conditions that many of the condemned faced. Despite the Supreme Court's positive rulings to provide due process protections for prisoners and several attempts to reform their more abusive practices, the prison population was growing at an increasingly rapid pace, leading to further deterioration in conditions.

During the time he began McMillian's case, Stevenson had been working on many cases for prisoners having to endure such horrible conditions and he was faced on a daily basis with such issues as inmate deaths, suicides, prisoner on prisoner violence, inadequate medical care, and staff and guard abuse.

All of this was swimming in his mind one evening as he drove home from Gadsden after dealing with a particularly taxing case there. He explains how he had been sitting in his car, parked outside of his apartment, trying to decompress after a long day. As he sat there, an Atlanta police car approached him and ordered him out of his car. As the altercation escalated and the officers pulled their weapons on him, the author was struck by how terrified he felt despite being completely innocent. The officers humiliated him in front of his neighbors, even going so far as to hold him against his car while they searched his vehicle. Eventually they revealed that they had been searching for a suspected criminal that had been burglarizing the neighborhood and they left him, embarrassed in the street, without apologizing.

The author explains that as he set out to write his official complaint to the Atlanta Police Department, he was struck by how much he felt like running the moment the officers drew their weapons. He realized that if he, a calm, intelligent, educated lawyer felt that fear to run from the police, what chance did other young black boys and men have if they were faced with the same situation? All the statistics and reports about black men being eight times more likely to be killed by police than white men began to make sense to him. He finished his complaint, taking care not to mention that he was a lawyer, filed it, and attempted to move on. Every few weeks, he explains, he would receive a letter claiming that the police were acting within the rights of their jobs. Displeased with being made to feel like he was the one at fault, Stevenson continued to appeal his complaint all the way up to the deputy chief of police. He received a half-hearted apology but found himself too busy with his own cases to continue his complaints any further.

He shares with the reader what he came out of the experience understanding. That situation was truly dangerous and ultimately unfair given that he was completely innocent but was likely targeted for simply being a black man. He closes this chapter by explaining how he was giving a talk in a small African American church one day about the challenges posed by the presumption of guilt assigned to certain social and racial groups. After his speech, an older black man approached him and thanked him for "beating the drum for justice." The man showed Stevenson several of the scars he obtained trying to fight for Civil Rights throughout the 1960's. This moment made the author realize that he had to do more, and keep fighting. He made the choice then to finally focus solely on opening his nonprofit office in Alabama.

Chapter Three: Trials and Tribulation

Stevenson returns to his narrative of Walter McMillian's arrest. As Sheriff Tate had not yet conducted an investigation into Myer's allegations regarding McMillian's involvement in the murder, Tate arrested McMillian on a pre textual charge of sodomy against Myers (a complete fabrication based solely on the officers' leading questioning of Myers during his initial testimony). Tate and the other officers threatened McMillian with lynching if he refused to admit his guilt in murdering Morrison. McMillian remained steadfast in his innocence in all allegations, so the officers placed him in jail until they could build a case.

Stevenson describes the flimsy testimony of Myers which involved McMillian randomly approaching him at a gas station and forcing him to drive him to the scene of the crime. While McMillian was in jail, the police took his truck to Bill Hooks, a jailhouse informant, and promised that he would be released from jail and given award money if he would connect McMillian's truck to the murder. Hooks invented a witness testimony to this and the state had enough to charge McMillian with capital murder.

The community was overwhelmed with relief over the announcement that someone had been charged with Morrison's murder and the police, particularly Sheriff Tate, were cheered as heroes. Despite all this, most members of the black community were shocked by the arrest and did their best to assert McMillian's innocence. Nearly all of his family, as well as several church members, could attest to his presence at a community barbeque during the time of the murder, giving him a solid alibi.

A few days before the capital murder charges, Myers recanted his testimony, but Sheriff Tate and the police ignored him, focusing instead on gaining more incriminating details from Myers. As Myers continued to deny, they turned to an unprecedented maneuver and threatened Myers and McMillian with death row. Stevenson explains that it is illegal to place someone who has not yet been tried for a crime in prison, let alone on death row. Yet, Sheriff Tate was able to convince the Holman Correctional Facility to house Myers and McMillian on death row in August of 1987, well before they were even given a trial.

Stevenson notes that nearly all of the death row prisoners were just as confused as McMillian was about why he was there, and many attempted to give him legal advice. His family scraped together money to hire the only black criminal lawyers in the region: J.L. Chestnut and Bruce Boynton. Despite their best efforts, they were unable to get McMillian released or transferred from Holman. While McMillian struggled with understanding who to trust or how to proceed, Myers fought with his own conflicts. Sitting on death row, Myers quickly understood that he had misplayed the police and was struggling to keep his advantages in the case. After an execution at the prison, Myers called Tate and told him that he would tell him anything if he could be taken off of death row. Myers was taken back to Monroe County and reaffirmed his initial testimony against McMillian. The DA used this testimony, as well as the one they had gathered from Hooks, to proceed with the case and set McMillian's trial for February 1988.

The district attorney Ted Pearson, the author explains, was approaching retirement and viewed the McMillian case as an opportunity to leave office with a very public victory. He was not at all deterred by the suspect nature of the testimonies against McMillian, nor by the doubts of the black community. What did concern him, however, was the Supreme Court's recent strides against a key feature of Southern trials: the all-white jury. Stevenson explains the history behind this trend and how a recent decision would likely lead McMillian's lawyers to object to a racially discriminatory jury selection.

Due to the publicity surrounding the case, McMillian's lawyers called for a change of venue and Pearson, with his own plan in mind, backed them up. The judge suggested a neighboring county and, in agreement with Pearson, it was decided that the trial be moved to Baldwin County, which had an African-

American population of only nine percent. This was disastrous for McMillian's case but they hoped that the evidence was enough to acquit him of the crime.

Myers once again recanted his testimony, this time waiting until the morning of the trial. This caused him to be sent, once again, to death row. After a few weeks, he was sent to the state hospital for the mentally ill when he began showing signs of severe emotional and psychological stress. After a thirty-day stint at the hospital, he was sent back to death row and Myers once again agreed to testify against McMillian. A new trial date was set for August 1988. The author summarizes this trial, explaining that after the lawyers made their arguments, it took the jury less than three hours to make their decision: Walter McMillian was guilty of the murder of Rhonda Morrison.

CHAPTER FOUR: THE OLD RUGGED

CROSS

Stevenson begins this chapter with just having opened his nonprofit law center, the Equal Justice Initiative (EJI) in Tuscaloosa, Alabama in February of 1989. In just the first few months they faced daunting obstacles such as the resignation of their first director, the withdrawal of support from University of Alabama, and the denial of funding from the state legislature. They faced a rash of new clients with upcoming execution dates due to the shift in the attorney general's office in seeking out executions of Alabama's condemned prisoners.

Stevenson visited death row every month and met with handfuls of new clients, all of whom selflessly begged for their help in preventing the upcoming May execution of Michael Lindsey. After Stevenson and EJI were unable to prevent his execution, the men then asked for their help in saving the next on the schedule, Horace Dunkins in July. The author details their attempts in saving these two men, noting in particular how they argued Dunkins's case. The EJI focused on how he suffered from mental retardation and made the point that executing people with intellectual disabilities was cruel and unusual punishment.

Following these two executions, the EJI moved to new offices in Montgomery and they received a call from another death row inmate, Herbert Richardson, whose execution date had been scheduled for August 18th, only two weeks from that call. Stevenson did his best to explain his current work situation to the man, and how he would be unable to take on the case. Yet, he came to realize that it was impossible to say no. Stevenson details Richardson's case, particularly how he was one of thousands of combat veterans who ended up in jail and his crime was likely a direct result of the PTSD he experienced from being in Vietnam.

He explains how he tried frantically to get a stay of execution, not on the grounds that Richardson was innocent (as his guilt was not really a question) but more that this case should not have been a capital murder case. Ultimately, the trial judge denied their request and Stevenson continued to file petitions all the way up until the actual day of execution. Only hours before Richardson was set to be executed, Stevenson heard back from the clerk of the Court that their final motion was denied. The author describes carrying out Richardson's final request to have "The Old Rugged Cross" play as he walked to the electric chair.

The author admits that this execution opened his eyes to a new way of viewing capital punishment. In debates afterwards, he would begin to argue that we do not think about the details of what killing someone involves and how it is just as cruel to put someone to death as it would be to rape, assault, or abuse them for their crime. In trying to reconcile himself to the realities of Richardson's death, he made updated plans for how to assist each of his clients in avoiding execution. He worked harder to recruit more staff for the EJI and obtain more support and resources. Despite feeling newly burdened by the perseverance

weight of everything, he knew that improvements were on the

horizon.

Bryant Stevenson demonstrated what
it means to persevere against all odds

CHAPTER FIVE: OF THE COMING OF JOHN

The author continues his narrative of McMillian's case by explaining that he traveled to Monroeville to meet with McMillian's family. He talked for a few hours with McMillian's wife and soon learned how the arrest burdened not only his family but the black community at large. Witnessing how this one miscarriage of justice could truly affect an entire community made the author more passionate to win the case. That same day he also met with most of McMillian's extended family, as well as nearly all the black members of the community who could testify to McMillian's alibi for that day.

Despite the stress of spending more time than ever at work and meeting with clients constantly, the author explains that spending time with McMillian was oddly comforting. The more time he spent with him, the more he realized just how kind and decent of a man McMillian truly was. Shortly after Stevenson met with the Monroeville family, he received a call from a man named Darnell Houston who claimed that he could prove McMillian's innocence. The author met him in person and Houston completely demolished Bill Hooks's testimony of seeing McMillian's truck that day. This reinforced the fact that so many of the State's key witnesses were unreliable, and yet, the court was believing their laughable testimonies.

The author's plan at this point was to appeal Walter's conviction to the Alabama Court of Criminal Appeals, hoping that the evidence against him was so unreliable that the conviction could be overturned. Using Houston's affidavit about Hooks's false testimony, he attempted to appeal to Tom Chapman, the new Monroe County district attorney. Shortly after speaking with the author, Houston was harassed and threatened with jail time by the police and prosecutors for even speaking with him. When the author heard this, he took on his case as well.

When the author met with Chapman, he was not reassured. Chapman seemed completely convinced of McMillian's guilt and even told him that he should not take on Houston's case. After making his personal feelings about the case clear, Chapman informed the author that his motion was denied. Stevenson was more frustrated than ever after speaking face to face with someone who saw the case so irrationally. The author realized that this went beyond a corruption of power. Everyone who was trying to help them was being threatened and he knew that this would make it impossible to prove McMillian's innocence. Feeling full of despair, Stevenson turned his attention to the next appeal.

CHAPTER SIX: SURELY DOOMED

Stevenson explains getting a call in 1990 from an elderly woman begging him to take on her fourteen year old grandson's case. While he could not commit to taking his death penalty case on—and did not believe that the child would be sent to death row as per rulings by the Supreme Court—he did promise to visit the boy. Arriving at the prison, Stevenson read the file on the juvenile and shares the details of the case with the reader. The boy, named Charlie, was charged with shooting and killing a man named George. The author describes the circumstances surrounding the crime, including the fact that George was Charlie's stepfather and not only had a history of abuse against his mother but, on the night of the murder, had beaten her close to death.

The author was positive that Charlie would not be prosecuted as an adult, but as he read the file further he discovered that George was a local police officer and the prosecution used this to get the maximum punishment for Charlie. Rather than being taken to juvenile jail, Charlie was taken to the county prison for adults. While in that jail, Charlie suffered constant physical and sexual abuse from the men around him. After many appeals, Stevenson was able to get Charlie transferred to a juvenile facility and downgraded his charge as a juvenile offense. Not only was Charlie released when he turned eighteen, but an elderly church couple heard Stevenson's story about Charlie during one of his speeches and decided to send him money to finance his college education. When he was released, this couple, and Charlie's mother showed up to take him home.

Chapter Seven: Justice Denied

The author returns again to the McMillian case and explains that their next appeal, the one outlining the insufficiency of the evidence, was denied. He was forced to admit that the courts were unwilling to see the mistakes they had made in the McMillian case. Their next plan was to ask the Court of Criminal Appeals to reconsider their decision, and if that did not work, they would seek review in the Alabama Supreme Court. McMillian, the author notes, was unrelentingly hopeful each step of the way and this helped the author to remain steadfast in his attempts.

They continued to investigate his case, hoping to find more evidence of his innocence, and they came across the county's financial records which showed that Bill Hooks was paid off by Sheriff Tate for his false testimony against McMillian. Hooks even had the charges that were against him dismissed in exchange for cooperation with the officers and the author discovered the paper trail that recorded all of it.

Stevenson points out that in the midst of all this new hopeful information, they received their biggest break in the case. Ralph Myers called the author and asked him to come visit him at the St. Clair Correctional Facility in Springville. During their visit, Myers completely recanted everything he had testified to at the trial. He claimed that group therapy in prison had made him want to come clean and he revealed it all: the pressure from the sheriff, being sent to death row because he did not want to cooperate, his own involvement in the Pittman murder and more. Before Stevenson and his partner Michael left, Myers warned them that they would be in physical danger if they actually learned the truth. On the way home, the two lawyers debate whether or not to believe Myers and decide to follow up on the leads that he provided.

First, they visited Kelly in the Tutwiler Prison for Women to see if Myers' story added up. She too admitted to framing Walter and confirmed Myer's false testimonies from before. After meeting with her, Stevenson and his partner looked further into the Pittman murder as a way to gain a new perspective on the coercion of Myers. In investigating the Pittman murder, they discovered several unanswered questions and met with her two aunts that had been desperately trying to solve the murder themselves for years. When they met with the two women, they voiced their suspicions about who they thought the murderer was and revealed their distrust of the local law enforcement. They explained that they were turned away by the police and even the state's victims' rights groups.

The author pauses the narrative here to explain why this might have happened. Social class has often had everything to do with which victims get more assistance and rights than others. Stevenson outlines many Supreme Court cases that attempted to protect victim's rights but how, ultimately, the criminal justice system obviously favored certain people over others. Pittman's aunts were of a lower social class, and thus received no assistance. Even further, families are often less likely to receive victim's rights if someone from that family has been previously incarcerated. After listening to their story,

Stevenson and his partner agreed to help them find out who murdered their niece.

After following up on the leads, and fully gathering all their new evidence, the EJI filed a Rule 31 petition that challenged the conviction on the basis of ineffective counsel, the State's failure to disclose evidence, and police and prosecutorial misconduct. It had been nearly three years since McMillian's first trial and he had spent most of that time on death row awaiting his execution date. The Baldwin County Circuit Court judge granted a review of their case and Stevenson had to meet once more with Tommy Chapman to gain the police and procedural files they would need for the review. When Stevenson and his partner arrived with a court order at Chapman's office, the DA was forthcoming with the files but very hostile. The files themselves were astonishing and it renewed their interest in helping solve the Pittman murder. This, as he explains, was right around when the EJI began to receive bomb threats.

CHAPTER EIGHT: ALL GOD'S CHILDREN

This chapter follows several juvenile cases that Stevenson took on during his time at the EJI. He details each case, noting in particular how certain physical, mental, and environmental factors led to the children being unable to understand the consequences of their actions. Sadly, all of these children were treated as adults and, rather than placed in juvenile jail, were convicted to the maximum: death row. He starts with Trina Gannett, who was convicted of second-degree murder and was committed to life in prison at the age of fourteen. He details the reasons why she should not have been convicted of such a crime and notes that she has been part of a the largest population of child offenders condemned to die in prison in the world.

Next, he examines Ian Manuel's case and how an accidental shooting led to him being sent to the toughest adult prison in Florida, despite only being thirteen years old. Next, he reviews

Antonio Nunez who, after surviving being shot, escaping South Central Los Angeles, and making a new life for himself, was sent back to his old gang infested neighborhoods by the California probation authorities. Eventually, he found himself convicted for aggravated kidnapping and attempted murder. At the age of fourteen, Nunez was the youngest person in the U.S. condemned to die in prison for a crime where no person was actually physically injured.

The author explains his inclusion of these stories to demonstrate that children who commit serious crimes are vulnerable to adult prosecution a lot more often than people believe. The politics of fear in the 1980s and 90s fueled mass incarceration and this trickled down to juvenile offenders. Many states, fearful of "super-predators" that the juvenile system could not handle, eliminated the minimum age for trying children as adults. As the juvenile population skyrocketed, the surgeon general was forced to admit their error in the "super-predator" myth in 2001, but the damage had already been done for many juvenile offenders.

Stevenson explains that he agreed to represent juveniles like this as a means to focus on challenging death-in-prison sentences imposed on children. This was but one of the major changes the EJI knew needed to be made in America, but it was a step. Eventually, they released a report that drew attention to the plight of the children sentenced to die in prison and this garnered more support for them to make a change. The author even shares a letter from Ian Manuel, thanking him and the EJI for all their help.

CHAPTER NINE: I'M HERE

This chapter begins with McMillian's hearing and the author notes how nervous he and his partner were about Myers's making his testimony. The man had recounted his story so many times, falling under the pressure from the State before, that they were nervous about his unpredictability. Before the hearing, the author explains that he had tried once more to reach out to Chapman to persuade him to reopen the investigation, but Chapman and the rest of the law enforcement were tired of the EJI's efforts. The author experienced so much hostility from them that he did not even feel he could report to the police the bomb and death threats they were receiving. Even the new judge on the case, Judge Thomas B. Norton, Jr., was irritated with the EJI after meeting with them during several pretrial hearings on different motions. The author admits that he suspected the Rule 32 hearing was only scheduled because they wanted the EJI and the McMillian case to go away.

The morning of the hearing they met with Myers and his demeanor did not do much to allay their fears. He was anxious and visibly distracted, but he wanted to continue on anyway. The author details the hearing, including the disheartening start when the judge allowed the State's crime investigators in the courtroom throughout the testimony. This was something that witnesses are not usually allowed to do as they may alter their testimony to fit with those of the other witnesses. Stevenson goes through Myers's testimony and notes how wonderful he was on the stand, surprising both himself and his partner, and heartening McMillian's relatives who watched in the audience. Stevenson details each witness that he called to the stand and which pieces of new evidence they offered towards McMillian's innocence. He notes how visibly affected Judge Norton seemed to have been as the hearing went on, his face revealing concern and confusion.

The next morning, Stevenson and his partner arrived at the courthouse early to find all of McMillian's relatives standing in the courthouse lobby. Apparently, they were not allowed inside the court, and when Stevenson approached the guard, he was almost not allowed in as well. After the confusion was cleared, the author explains that the State had allowed more than half of their audience in before McMillian's and added new security measures such as a metal detector and a German Sheppard. When confronted about this, Chapman claimed that McMillian's supporters did not arrive early enough, but the author could tell it was another effort to confuse matters in the hearing.

Despite this minor setback, the author describes that day in court as having gone very well. As they presented the evidence, it seemed that the State's audience were also feeling more confused towards McMillian's guilt. The next day, very few people showed up to support the State and Stevenson took this as a good sign of their efforts. He shares an anecdote about one of McMillian's supporters—Mrs. Williams—who was so frightened by the guard dog in the court, that she missed the second day's proceedings. Later it was explained to the author that she had endured a bad experience with police dogs during the Civil Rights Movement. The third day, however, Mrs. Williams gathered all the courage she had and proudly made it past the dogs and into the court room. She proclaimed exuberantly, "I ain't scared of no dog!" The author uses this anecdote as a metaphor for the courage it took all involved to stand up against the injustices being done by the court.

As the author closes his recollection of the hearing, he explains that they saved the most powerful evidence for last. This was the tapes that were recorded when Sheriff Tate and the other officers first interrogated Myers and they demonstrated how the officers threatened and forced him to come up with his false testimony against McMillian. This, once and for all, proved corruption and the false testimony of Myers. After three days, the proceedings were adjourned and Stevenson and his partner anxiously awaited the judge's decision.

CHAPTER TEN: MITIGATION

This chapter focuses mostly on how American prisons have become warehouses for the mentally ill. The author explains that misguided drug policy, excessive sentencing, and reform on institutionalization have largely been the causes for this. He details the deinstitutionalization laws of the 1960s and 70s and shows a direct correlation to mass imprisonment, particularly of people suffering from mental disabilities. Over 50 percent of inmates in the U.S. today have a diagnosed mental illness.

Stevenson next examines several people he has represented that fit this sad statistic, including Avery Jenkins and George Daniel. He details each of their cases, including the crimes they committed and the convictions they received. The most horrific part of their stories is how they were treated in jail and how their disabilities grew much worse as a result of their incarceration. Stevenson even unmasks a few uncredentialed doctors, such as Dr. Ed Seger, who falsified their degrees and worked in hospitals and prisons misdiagnosing people.

The author shares one anecdote from when he went to visit Jenkins in prison and was confronted by a hostile and obviously racist guard. Every time he went in to visit his client, he was forced by this guard to undergo unnecessary measures such as intense documentation and strip searching. After Jenkins's hearing, in which they were able to prove his disabilities, Stevenson once again visited his client before they received the news.

When he encountered the guard this time, however, he was treated with much more respect. It turns out that the guard was moved by Stevenson's argument, particularly because he too was a victim of an abusive foster home and much of his anger stemmed from that. The guard apologized to the author and this anecdote serves to demonstrate the main point that sometimes our judicial system does not always produce the same kind of mercy that human beings are capable of. In closing the chapter, he reveals that they won Jenkins's trial and got him off of death row and into a proper mental health facility.

Chapter Eleven: I'll Fly Away

Stevenson begins the chapter a month after the McMillian hearing with their law office still receiving bomb and death threats. It escalated to the point where he began receiving threatening calls at home as well. All of the tension came to a head when the EJI finally received a fax detailing the judge's ruling on McMillian's hearing: denied. While the author admits to anticipating this ruling, he found the superficiality of the court's reasoning upsetting. He shares the text of the fax for the readers to see this for themselves.

Their next step was to go to the appellate court. By now the author was beginning to become something of an expert at filing death penalty appeals and, since his first hearing for McMillian, he and the EJI won 16 death penalty reversals. So many people began reaching out to the EJI for relief that they were able to expand their offices and hire more employees. All the while, Stevenson remained dedicated to McMillian's case.

His next chief concern was to encourage the belief of McMillian's innocence in his own hometown in preparation for his return. The author points out the dangers of media: too much can exacerbate a case, and even anger a judge—as was the case with their own Judge Patterson who had famously sued *The New York Times*. Yet, the author knew that he could use the media to help give the community a more informed view of McMillian's innocence and how much he had suffered over the injustice of his conviction.

Stevenson describes how a little bit of media coverage led into more and more until, eventually, *60 Minutes* wanted to do a piece on the McMillian case. Their reporter interviewed many of the people whose testimonies were presented at the hearing. They interviewed Chapman, who claimed that it was silly to suggest that there was any racial bias in this case: McMillian was simply guilty. When the piece aired the local officers attempted to discredit it. Even the local media and some influential community leaders joined in as they felt they were unfairly portrayed by the story that was presented by the show. Yet, the black community was thrilled to finally see some honest coverage of the case. The *60 Minutes* coverage also began to make Chapman wonder about the reliability of the evidence against McMillian and he finally began to realize how damaging it could be to be the face of defending the conviction. Privately, he hired investigators to conduct another examination into McMillian's guilt.

These new investigators, Tom Taylor and Greg Cole, called Stevenson, asking if he would share some of the case files the EJI had been gathering for their evidence. The more they worked together, the more these new investigators became convinced of McMillian's innocence. Six months after their appeal, Taylor and Cole called the EJI and asked to meet to discuss their findings. They outright stated that there was no way McMillian could have murdered Morrison and that they were going to report this to the attorney general and district attorney. Even further, they wanted to set out to discover who actually did commit the murder, hoping that this could help prove McMillian's innocence and bring an end to the case altogether.

Stevenson admits that he and his partner did have a suspect in mind when it came to Morrison's killer. Witnesses pointed out a white man around the scene of the crime shortly after the murders and the EJI was contacted by a man who fit the witnesses' descriptions asking a lot of questions about Morrison's death. They shared this information with Taylor and Cole. After meeting with these new investigators, Stevenson was able to use their involvement to file an appeal that claimed that the overwhelming evidence in the case entitled McMillian to immediate relief and release from prison. Six weeks after this, the clerk of the court called the EJI to share the ruling: McMillian was innocent and would be released.

The author explains how things moved quickly after that. Surprisingly, Chapman wanted to work with the EJI to help file a motion to dismiss all charges against McMillian. The hearing on this motion was short and sweet and McMillian and his family were ecstatic with happiness. The author, however, found himself surprisingly angry. He thought about all the unnecessary pain and suffering that McMillian had endured and how thousands more innocent people were still incarcerated and would likely not receive the same help or relief. In closing the hearing, Stevenson addressed his concerns to the court and noted how much work must be done to our judicial system to stop injustices such as this from ever occurring again.

Chapter Twelve: Mother, Mother

This chapter focuses solely on another subsect of prisoners unjustly incarcerated: women labeled as "dangerous mothers." He tells the story of Marsha Colbey, a woman who found herself imprisoned at the Tutwiler Prison for Women when she was convicted for capital murder of her still-born baby. Stevenson gives a detailed background on Colbey, noting in particular how she was of a poor, lower class and had been a former drug addict. At the age of forty-three, she was pregnant with her seventh child but she did not have the time, money, or resources to stop working or get the medicine and vitamins she needed. She birthed the baby one day while she was taking a bath and the son was stillborn.

A neighbor noticed the small grave marker they had dug for their child and, knowing Colbey's past drug issues, reported her to the police. Kathleen Enstice, a forensic pathologist, testified that the baby had been born alive—yet later admitted that there was no way for her to actually determine this from the baby's exhumed body. In fact, all of Enstice's conclusions about Colbey's "murder" of her son were later discredited by many medical experts, but her testimony was used in the prosecution against Colbey. The media picked up the story and the recent wave of "dangerous mother" stories in the news exacerbated the case.

The author explains the laws and court cases that led to convictions of women such as Colbey. From "dangerous environment" laws to "child chemical endangerment" statutes, these laws were meant to protect children from truly dangerous households. Eventually, these laws were applied much more broadly and were used to convict many of the poor and marginalized. Colbey herself fell victim to these laws and was sentenced to life imprisonment without the possibility for parole.

Stevenson provides a graphic and detailed description of the deplorable conditions at the Tutwiler Prison for Women. He explains how winning the case of one of the women from that prison led to the EJI meeting and representing Colbey. In working on her case, as well as those of several other women prisoners at Tutwiler, they uncovered horrific accounts of sexual abuse and rape of the female prisoners. In addition to working on Colbey's case, the EJI also tried to fight against the sexual violence at Tutwiler.

The extent of the appeals and motions in Colbey's case were just as lengthy as those with McMillian's and it took nearly three full years to settle her case and reward her full credit for ten years of wrongful imprisonment. Stevenson ends the chapter with Colbey attending the EJI's yearly benefit dinner in New York City where she was honored for her own advocating for the rights of female prisoners.

CHAPTER THIRTEEN: RECOVERY

The author describes what occurred after McMillian's release, including a *New York Times* article about the trial and floods of television and newspaper interviews. The author explains that he encouraged the media coverage because he felt that if the citizens of Monroe county heard enough media about McMillian's innocence, they would be more likely to welcome him home. Stevenson and McMillian traveled across the U.S. speaking at legal conferences and they even held a hearing with the U.S. Senate Judiciary Committee regarding the death penalty. McMillian was eager to participate as he hoped that sharing his experience could be prevented this from happening to others.

After his release, McMillian heeded the author's warnings about death threats and lived with his sister in Florida for a few months. Eventually, McMillian's longing to return home proved too strong and he resettled in a trailer on the property he owned in Monroe County. He returned to his logging business while the EJI busied themselves with filing a civil lawsuit against his wrongful prosecution and conviction. Alabama was not one of the ten states that offered aid to innocent people released from prison, so they sought out the assistance of a local legislator who introduced a bill on McMillian's behalf. This went nowhere, but the media picked it up and misreported an extravagant payoff. This error did nothing more than to create outrage and suspicion from McMillian's neighbors and many began harassing him for financial help.

The author details the many steps they took to get McMillian assistance and it took nearly a year before they reached a settlement for a few hundred thousand dollars. He also explains that their claim against Sheriff Tate's misconduct was ruled down and Tate continues to be sheriff to this day, going on in this role for more than twenty-five years.

Shortly after all this, McMillian suffered a severe injury at work and was forced to move in with Stevenson while he recovered and gained mobility. The author notes that despite this obvious setback, McMillian remained unwaveringly upbeat. He switched careers, deciding to pursue the junk business which would require much less physical exertion on his part.

The author shares the many times he and McMillian worked together to spread awareness of wrongful imprisonment, including attending a national conference for exonerated former death row prisoners in 1998. Around this time, Stevenson was contacted by the Swedish Ambassador to the United States and was told that the EJI was selected for a prestigious Swedish human rights award. He was interviewed by Swedish media and had them visit and interview McMillian as well. As the author was in Stockholm to receive the award, he saw their interviews on their local news and watched as McMillian became uncharacteristically emotional in front of the camera. McMillian sobbed violently and described all the damages that he had endured and the suffering that came out of his own wrongful conviction. The author decided to head back to Alabama as soon as possible to see McMillian in person.

CHAPTER FOURTEEN: CRUEL AND UNUSUAL

This chapter returns to the concern of the author's regarding unlawful prosecution of minors. He begins with an anecdote about thirteen year old Joe Sullivan who was convicted in adult court for sexual battery when he had been caught during a burglary with his two friends. Sullivan, he points out, suffered from mental disabilities, read at a first-grade level, and experienced repeated physical abuse from his father. He was sentenced to life imprisonment without the possibility of parole and was sent to an adult prison. For eighteen years he was subjected to sexual violence, rape, and other traumas that led to several suicide attempts, multiple sclerosis and confinement to a wheelchair.

The EJI was made known of Sullivan's case in 2007 and they decided to challenge his death in prison sentence as unconstitutionally cruel and unusual punishment. Somehow the State had destroyed the DNA evidence that would have proved his innocence and his two friends, his co-defendants, had died, leaving no other witnesses who could testify on his behalf. Because the Supreme Court had banned the death penalty for juveniles in 2005, they tried to figure out how to use that constitutional reasoning as a legal basis for their challenge.

The author takes a moment here to explain the irony of him becoming involved in cases of teenagers who committed violent crimes. When he was sixteen years old, his grandfather was stabbed to death by several teens who had broken into his apartment in the South Philadelphia housing projects. Back then, he found it hard to understand why someone could be so pointlessly destructive. Decades later, he explains, he was beginning to understand that the lives that these children endured had a lot to do with their actions. The way that these teenagers developed biologically and psychosocially were a direct result of their environment, and often they lacked the maturity and independence to have the proper judgement in these situations.

The EJI argued that young adolescents lack the life experience and background knowledge to inform their choices. Combining this with the environments that many of these children come from, it makes them vulnerable to the poor decision making that often leads to violent situations. They connected the ban on the death penalty to death in prison sentences as they are also unchangeable, once and for all judgments on these children's entire lives. Children below a certain age are unfinished products and their potential for growth beyond their one bad decision is enormous.

Initially, their arguments were met with little success until May 2009, when the Supreme Court agreed to review the case. They decided to review Sullivan's case as well as that of another sixteen year old named Terrance Graham. After the briefs were filed, Stevenson traveled to Washington in November to speak before the Supreme Court. The court was packed with media and his arguments were met with uncertainty, making it difficult for him to predict what the verdict would be. After his argument, he visited Sullivan in prison where the young boy shared with him a poem he wrote about being a good person.

CHAPTER FIFTEEN: BROKEN

This chapter focuses on McMillian and his general decline in health after his interview with the Swedish media. McMillian demonstrated signs of dementia and one day he collapsed and was taken to a hospital in Mobile. The hospital contacted the author and they explained the extent of McMillian's illness and that he would require constant care. Sadly, most places that cared for the elderly and infirm would not take people convicted of a felony, so they had to hire a social worker to find a suitable place for him.

Meanwhile, the EJI had a huge workload and they were still awaiting the verdict from their Supreme Court argument in the Sullivan case. Even further, the Alabama Supreme Court had just begun to schedule execution dates for several death row prisoners who had just completed their appeals. The EJI agreed to take on all their cases and this doubled their caseload. In between, Stevenson found time to visit McMillian in the care facility they found for him and, sadly, McMillian believed that he was on death row again. As the author was leaving his visit with McMillian, he received news that the Alabama Supreme Court had just scheduled another execution. The pressure for the EJI to succeed was higher than ever as Alabama, at the time, had the nation's highest execution rate per capita and they were scrambling to keep up.

Between these cases and taking on new challenges, like arguing against the constitutionality of lethal injection protocols, the author was having difficulty managing it all. By the time McMillian was forced out of his care facility and the EJI took on a client whose execution was in thirty days, Stevenson was beyond coping. When he found out that the court once again denied that client's stay of execution and would be put to death in less than hour, the author's heart was completely broken. He describes sitting in his office being surrounded by the files of tragic stories and misery. He felt full of brokenness: the broken justice system, the broken clients, and the broken state. He was ready to give it all up once and for all.

As he looked around his office once more and saw the list of the EJI's staff, which had grown to nearly forty people, he realized that he could not just leave. After twenty-five years of this work, he explains, he realized he did this because he was broken, too. His own struggles against inequality, poverty, oppression and injustice left him just as broken as his clients. But that was why he felt he needed to fight for them. They shared the condition of brokenness and this connected them. It made him want to seek mercy for his clients that much more.

Thinking about this, as well as of all the ways in which the justice system has legalized vengeful and cruel punishment made him feel stronger. He realized that if we could all own up to our own weaknesses and fears, we would not want to kill the broken amongst us. We would look harder for solutions and to care for those among us that are disabled, abused, and neglected. He shares an anecdote from when he once met Rosa Parks. When asked what he did, he went off on a tirade about what he and the EJI did. After it all, Ms. Parks simply said,

"Tired, tired, tired." It all made her so tired. But, she explained, that was why he had to be "brave, brave, brave." This, he explains, is the power of mercy. It belongs to the undeserving and it is strong enough to break the cycle of victimization. He vowed that he would stay brave and continue to seek out mercy for those who truly needed it.

CHAPTER SIXTEEN: THE STONECATCHERS' SONG OF SORROW

It was on May 17, 2010, when he received the Supreme Court's ruling that life imprisonment without parole for children was cruel and unusual punishment. Two years after this, the EJI also won a constitutional ban on these same kinds of sentences imposed on children convicted of homicides. Many of their cases were being reviewed by the courts and over two thousand people condemned for these crimes as children became eligible for relief and reduced sentences.

The EJI continued their work, focusing on banning the housing of children under the age of eighteen in adult prisons and then, eventually, on trying children in adult courts. Their death penalty work had won relief for over a hundred prisoners and, starting in 2012, they had eighteen months of no executions in Alabama. The nationwide rate of mass incarceration slowed and, in 2012, the U.S. saw the first decline in prison population in decades.

The author and his colleagues decided to turn the EJI's work towards race and poverty. He details why he know understands that most of the worst thinking about justice is steeped in myths of racial difference. He points to four institutions that have shaped our approach to race and justice but have also been severely misunderstood: slavery, the collapse of Reconstruction, Jim Crow laws, and mass incarceration. He feels that, finally, the EJI has been able to address some of the issues caused by these institutions.

Their successes have also led to bigger problems, Stevenson points out. The Supreme Court rulings they earned now entitled hundreds of people to new sentences and many have been left with no lawyers to assist them. The EJI ended up taking on nearly a hundred new cases after the court's "cruel and unusual" decision in 2010. After the second ban, they took on a hundred more. While overwhelming, the author highlights how truly rewarding the work has been. He ends the chapter with another story of their success. After arguing a case for a man who spent decades in prison, the judge released the man immediately and the people in the courtroom erupted

in jubilant applause for the just decision.

EPILOGUE

Walter McMillian died on September 11, 2013. At his funeral at Limestone Faulk A.M.E. Zion Church in Monroeville, the author spoke about what McMillian had taught him. He helped Stevenson understand why they needed to reform a system of criminal justice that treats the rich and guilty better than the poor and innocent. He told them that, more than anything, McMillian taught him that mercy is just when it is rooted in hopefulness. The people who have not necessarily earned mercy are often the most meaningful recipients. McMillian always forgave those who treated him unjustly and, in the end, his own just mercy towards others allowed him to recover and live a life that was worth celebrating

ANALYSIS

This work offers a firsthand look at how complicated the justice system is for certain racial and socioeconomic groups. Stevenson's casework and social activism allow the reader an unpolished view of how these prisoners are misjudged and incorrectly convicted. He backs up his arguments with solid legal research and data that he has used to prove the layers of injustice hiding behind many of the courts' convictions, particularly those involving the death penalty.

A strength of the book is the first hand experience the author is able to provide. Not only has he been the lawyer defending the fates of these wrongfully convicted prisoners, but he has also been misjudged himself. He shares his own experiences as a black man in America and how, despite being a law-abiding and well-educated citizen, he has endured prejudices similar to those felt by his own clients. This connection to his work makes him passionate and that truly shines throughout the novel. This helps to make his message that much more powerful for the reader.

There is very little to criticize about this book. The very point of the novel is to reveal the unfairness behind how certain people are convicted in the American justice system and the author truly does his best to show the effects on all manners of people. At times, it could be said that he does not show both sides of each trial, portraying members of law enforcement and the court as somewhat one-dimensional villains. This is likely due to his steadfast focus on those victimized by the system, not leaving a lot of time or attention to fully characterize the people on the other side of the trials.

The author's credibility is without question as he has been the face of social activism for the unjustly convicted for over 25 years. As the founder of the EJI, he has helped find relief and reduced sentences for hundreds of prisoners. All of this experience allows him to speak expertly on the criminal justice system and the cases he has tried. It also gives the reader an inside look into how the system has been corrupted and what it has taken to bring about change.

What the reader can take from the book is a different look at people we often dismiss as mere criminals. Yes, many of these people have made mistakes and committed crimes, but they are also victims in their own right. The brokenness that all these people share in how they have been mistreated by the criminal justice system humanizes them. The author fights so passionately for them because he knows they deserve just as many human rights as we do. In sharing their cases, and their stories, he hopes that his audience will come to see the justice in allowing them mercy.

37086509R00044

Made in the USA
Middletown, DE
21 February 2019